THIRTY OBI

WIS

SELECTED BY MATTHEW ENGEL

PENGUIN BOOKS

PENGUIN BOOKS

Published by the Penguin Group. Penguin Books Ltd, 27 Wrights Lane, London
w8 5tz, England. Penguin Books USA Inc., 375 Hudson Street, New York,
New York 10014, USA. Penguin Books Australia Ltd, Ringwood, Victoria, Australia.
Penguin Books Canada Ltd, 10 Alcorn Avenue, Toronto, Ontario, Canada m4v 3b2.
Penguin Books (NZ) Ltd, 182–190 Wairau Road, Auckland 10, New Zealand · Penguin
Books Ltd, Registered Offices: Harmondsworth, Middlesex, England · These
extracts are from various editions of *Wisden Cricketers' Almanack*. This edition published 1996. This collection copyright © John Wisden & Co. Ltd, 1996 · 'Wisden'
and its woodcut device are registered trademarks of John Wisden & Co. Ltd · All
rights reserved · Typeset by Rowland Phototypesetting Ltd, Bury St Edmunds,
Suffolk. Printed in England by Clays Ltd, St Ives plc · Except in the United States
of America, this book is sold subject to the condition that it shall not, by way of
trade or otherwise, be lent, re-sold, hired out, or otherwise circulated without the
publisher's prior consent in any form of binding or cover other than that in which it
is published and without a similar condition including this condition being imposed
on the subsequent purchaser · 10 9 8 7 6 5 4 3 2 1

A new edition of *Wisden Cricketers' Almanack* is published each April.

CONTENTS

Introduction

Wisden Cricketers' Almanack was founded in 1864. In 1892 it began printing obituaries. In a period of just over a century, *Wisden* has published around ten thousand of them. Traditionally these have been something far more than a mere chronicle of cricketing achievements and have emphasized the extent to which the game is just part of a life.

The *Almanack* has marked the passing of all the great figures of cricket, many of the lesser figures, and some of the great figures of the outside world who have had a connection with the game. This is a small selection of people in all three categories. The obituaries have been described as a miniature social history of England. They certainly form a history of literary styles.

Some of these are signed, and constitute very personal appreciations. Others are unsigned; and the modern *Almanack*'s policy is that, as in the very early days, obituaries should be anonymous – but never flavourless.

MATTHEW ENGEL, Editor, *Wisden Cricketers' Almanack*

MANNING, CARDINAL, died on January 14, 1892, aged 83. It may seem a little strange to include Cardinal Manning's name in a cricket obituary, but inasmuch as he played for Harrow against Winchester at Lord's in 1825, in the first match that ever took place between the two schools, his claim cannot be disputed.

(*Wisden* 1893)

GALE, FREDERICK, well known to thousands of cricketers under his nom de plume 'The Old Buffer', died on April 24, 1904, in the Charterhouse. Born in 1823, he had lived to a ripe old age. He was in the Winchester XI in 1841, and appeared at Lord's that year against both Harrow and Eton. Winchester suffered a single-innings' defeat at the hands of Harrow, but beat Eton by 109 runs. The victory was one to be proud of, as the Eton team included Emilius Bayley, Walter Marcon, George Yonge, and Harvey Fellows. Mr Gale did not win fame as a player, but no one loved cricket more than he did, or supported it more keenly. He kept up his enthusiasm to the end, and even so recently as the season of 1903 he was to be seen at the Oval – bent in figure, but still full of vivacity. As a writer on the game he was prolific, several books and numberless magazine and newspaper articles coming from his pen. He lived for a good many years at Mitcham, and in those days took the liveliest interest in young Surrey players, delighting in the triumphs of Jupp, Tom Humphrey, and, a little later, Richard Humphrey. A special protégé of his was George Jones, who bowled for Surrey more than twenty years ago, when the county's fortunes were at a low ebb. Mr Gale had a high ideal of the way in which cricket should be played, and in his various writings always insisted on the necessity of good fielding. His particular aversion was the batsman who played for his average rather than for his side. Like many old men, he had an abiding regard for the heroes of his youth, and nothing pleased him better, when he found a congenial listener, than to talk about Fuller Pilch, Hillyer, and Felix. Still, he could be just as enthusiastic when discussing the batting of W. G. Grace and the bowling of Alfred Shaw. He enjoyed the friendship of John Ruskin, and took the famous writer to the Oval in 1882 to see the Australians.

(*Wisden* 1905)

HEMINGWAY, GEORGE EDWARD, a brother of Messrs W. M'G. and R. E. Hemingway, died at Rangoon on March 11, 1907. He was born at Macclesfield in 1872, was in the Uppingham XI in 1888, and in 1898 appeared for Gloucestershire against Yorkshire, at Sheffield. He was a free batsman and in the field generally stood mid-off or cover-point, but business and weak sight handicapped his play considerably. On one occasion, when playing a single-wicket match against his two brothers, he hit the ball into a bed of nettles; the fieldsmen quarrelled as to who should recover it, and during the argument the batsman ran about 250.

(*Wisden* 1908)

OATES, CAPT. LAWRENCE EDWARD GRACE, who died on March 17, 1912, his thirty-second birthday, whilst returning from the South Pole with Capt. Scott's ill-fated party, played cricket for his House as a lower boy at Eton.

(Wisden 1914)

W. G. GRACE
WILLIAM GILBERT GRACE, BORN AT DOWNEND, NEAR BRISTOL, JULY 18, 1848
DIED AT HIS HOME, FAIRMOUNT, ELTHAM, KENT, OCTOBER 23, 1915

In no branch of sport has anyone ever enjoyed such an unquestioned supremacy as that of W. G. Grace in the cricket field. In his great days he stood alone, without a rival. Not even George Fordham and Fred Archer as jockeys, or John Roberts as a billiard player, had such a marked superiority over the men who were nearest to them in point of ability. Whatever may be in store for the game of cricket in the future it seems safe to say that such a player will never be seen again. A rare combination of qualities went to the making of W. G. Grace. Blessed with great physical advantages, he united to a strength of constitution that defied fatigue a devotion to the game which time was powerless to affect. When he was in his prime no sun was too hot and no day too long for him. It is on record that when, for a cricketer, he was no longer young, he spent the whole night by the bedside of a patient, and on the following day stepped on to the Clifton College ground and scored over 200 runs.

Mr Grace's career in the cricket field – almost unexampled in point of length – can be sharply divided into two portions. His early fame as a batsman culminated in the season of 1876, when in the month of August he scored in three successive innings, 344 against Kent at Canterbury, 177 against Notts at Clifton, and 318 not out against Yorkshire at Cheltenham. Soon after that, having passed his examination at Edinburgh as a surgeon, he thought of gradually retiring from cricket and settling down, like his elder brothers, to the busy life of a general practitioner. As a matter of fact, he did for many years hold a parish appointment at Bristol, a locum tenens doing his work in the summer months. There can be little doubt that his change of plans was mainly due to the appearance in England in 1878 of the first Australian XI. Those whose memories go back to that now somewhat distant time will remember the tremendous sensation caused by the victories of that XI, and in particular by Spofforth's bowling, and Blackham's wicket-keeping. Englishmen realised, with an excusable shock of surprise, that in the cricket field there were serious rivals to be faced.

Mr Grace had never been in such poor batting form as he was in 1878, and on the few occasions that he met the Australian bowlers he did nothing in the least degree worthy of his reputation. I have no exact knowledge on the point, but I feel tolerably certain that the success of the Australians revived Mr Grace's ambition. At any rate, the fact remains that, though the most brilliant part of his career had ended before the invasion of 1878, the Australians found him for the best part of twenty years the most formidable of their opponents. This second part of his career as a batsman began towards the end of the season of 1880. Following some fine performances for Gloucestershire he played, as everyone will remember, a great innings of 152 at the Oval in the first match in this country between England and Australia. Even then, however, though only in his thirty-third year, he laboured under one serious disadvantage. In the four years following his triumphs of 1876, he had put on a lot of weight and was very heavy for so young a man.

He said himself at the time that he was never in better form than in those closing weeks of the season of 1880, and that, but for lack of condition, he would have made many more runs. Against increasing bulk he had to battle for the rest of his cricket life. For a long time he retained his activity to a surprising extent, but as the years went on his once splendid fielding gradually left him. He kept up his batting, however, in a marvellous way, the success of what one may call his second period in the cricket field reaching its climax when in 1895 he scored a thousand runs in first-class cricket in the month of May. His batting at that time has never been approached by a man of the same age; he was nearly 47. In 1896 he was still very good, but after that the years began to tell on him, and in 1899, when he moved from Bristol to the Crystal Palace, he played at Trent Bridge his last match for England against Australia. Still, though he had now done with Test matches, he went on playing first-class cricket for several seasons, his career practically ending with the Gentlemen and Players' match at the Oval in 1906. The finish was worthy of him as, on his fifty-eighth birthday, he scored 74, batting up to a certain point with much of the vigour of his younger days.

Of Mr Grace's cricket from the time of his first appearance at Lord's in July, 1864, for the South Wales Club against the MCC down to the end of 1876, columns could be written without exhausting the subject. He was picked for the Gentlemen, as a lad of 17, both at Lord's and the Oval in 1865, the honour being conferred upon him quite as much for his medium-pace bowling as for his batting. A year later, however, he proved himself, beyond all question, the best batsman in England, two wonderful innings at the Oval establishing his fame. He scored 224 not out for England

5

against Surrey and 173 not out for Gentlemen of the South against Players of the South. An attack of scarlet fever interfered with his cricket in 1867, but after that he never looked back. His best seasons as a batsman were, I fancy, 1871, 1873, and 1876. His play in 1871 far surpassed anything that had ever been done before.

In his whole career he scored in Gentlemen and Players' matches 6,008 runs with an average of 42 and took 271 wickets for a trifle under 19 runs each. He made seven hundreds for the Gentlemen at Lord's, four at the Oval, and one each at Brighton, Prince's, Scarborough, and Hastings. The first of his seven hundreds at Lord's was obtained in 1868, and the last, after an interval of 27 years, in 1895. Of these seven innings the first was, perhaps, the most remarkable. Going in first wicket down for a very strong side he took out his bat for 134, the total only reaching 201. As Lord Harris has pointed out the wickets at Lord's in those far-off days were by no means so true and easy as careful attention made them in later years. A score of a hundred at Lord's in the '60s against the best bowling was an incomparably bigger feat than it is at the present time.

No mention has yet been made of Mr Grace's connection with Gloucestershire cricket. With his two brothers, E. M. and G. F., and other fine, though less gifted, players to help him, he built up a team of remarkable strength in batting and fielding. The County Club was established in 1871, and in 1876 and 1877 the XI stood ahead of all rivals. Until beaten at Clifton by the first Australian XI in 1878 the team never lost a match at home. After G. F. Grace's death in 1880, Gloucestershire never seemed quite the same as before, but in 1885, and again in 1898, there was, thanks to W. G.'s batting and C. L. Townsend's bowling, a brief revival of old glories. The Gloucestershire matches at Clifton and Cheltenham in the old days were delightful, the Gloucestershire XI being quite a family party. Like other families they had their little differences of opinion, but there was a great feeling of comradeship among them, and they played cricket with tremendous zest.

Mr Grace's venture in connection with the London County at the Crystal Palace did not add to his fame. He was in his fifty-first year when he left Bristol, the experiment being made far too late. Many pleasant matches were played at the Palace, but they were carried through in too leisurely a spirit to appeal to a public brought up on cricket of a much sterner character. If tried fifteen years earlier the project might have proved a success. As it was the London County faded out when Mr Grace's contract with the Crystal Palace Company came to an end.

With Mr Grace's characteristics as a batsman I must deal rather briefly. He was, in the main, quite orthodox in style, his bat being as perfectly straight as Fuller Pilch's, but he greatly enlarged the domain of orthodoxy, playing a far more aggressive and punishing game than any of the classic batsmen who came before him. It should be explained here that E. M. Grace, who first made the family name famous, played a game of his own and was a little outside comparisons. W. G. developed the art of batting to an extraordinary degree, but he was not, like E. M., a revolutionist. There is his own authority for stating that he did not indulge in the pull till he was 40. A splendid all-round hitter, he excelled all his predecessors in his power of placing the ball on the on-side. A story is told of a cricketer who had regarded Fuller Pilch as the last word in batting, being taken in his old age to see Mr Grace bat for the first time. He watched the great man for a quarter of an hour or so and then broke out into expressions of boundless delight. 'Why,' he said, 'this man scores continually from balls that old Fuller would have been thankful to stop.' The words conveyed everything. Mr Grace when he went out at the ball did 7 so for the purpose of getting runs. Pilch and his imitators, on the other hand, constantly used forward play for defence alone.

When the wicket was difficult and the ball turning, Mr Grace trusted for defence to that strong back play which, even in his boyhood, convinced his people at home that he would be a greater batsman than his brother, E. M. Mr Grace's batting from 1868 onwards quite overshadowed his bowling, and yet during his career he took many hundreds of wickets. Indeed, old Bob Thoms, the umpire, always contended that if he had not been such a wonderful batsman he would have been the best slow bowler in England. Even as it was he held his own very well with such masters as Alfred Shaw and Southerton. He bowled medium pace with a purely round arm action in his young days, but slackened his speed about 1872.

His superb strength and health enabled him to stand any amount of cricket, but in his best two years as a bowler – 1875 and 1877 – his batting fell off fifty per cent. He did not rely much on break, only turning in a little from leg, but he had great command over his length and very seldom indeed pitched short. His chief strength lay in head work. No one was quicker to find out the weak points of a batsman or more certain to lure an impetuous hitter to his doom. In Gloucestershire's great days he was much helped by brilliant fielding, Fred Grace in particular, at deep square leg, being invaluable to him. When he first appeared for the Gentlemen, Mr Grace was a splendid outfield, capable of throwing the ball 100 yd., but as time went on he took to fielding near the wicket and for many years he had no superior at point except his brother E. M.

Personally, W. G. struck me as the most natural and unspoiled of men. Whenever and wherever one met him he was always the same. There was not the smallest trace of affectation about him. If anything annoyed him he was quick to show anger, but his little outbursts were soon over. One word I will add. No man who ever won such world-wide fame could have been more modest in speaking of his own doings. Mr Grace was married in 1873 to Miss Agnes Day. His domestic life was unclouded except by the death of his only daughter in 1899 and of his eldest son in 1905. Mrs Grace and two sons – Captain H. E. Grace, RN, and Captain C. B. Grace, KFRE – survive him.

(Wisden 1916)

JEEVES, PERCY (Royal Warwickshire Regiment), was killed on July 22, 1916, England losing a cricketer of whom very high hopes had been entertained. Jeeves was born at Earlsheaton, in Yorkshire, on March 5, 1888. He played his first serious cricket for the Goole CC, and became a professional at Hawes. He took part in Yorkshire trial matches in 1910, but presumably failed to attract much attention. Soon afterwards he went to live in Warwickshire, playing for that county, when not fully qualified, against the Australians and South Africans in 1912. No special success rewarded him in those matches, but in 1913 he did brilliant work for Warwickshire, both as bowler and batsman, and firmly established his position. He took 106 wickets in first-class matches that season at a cost of 20.88 each, and scored 765 runs with an average of 20.13. In 1914 he held his own as a bowler, taking 90 wickets in first-class matches, but in batting he was less successful than before. He was chosen for Players against Gentlemen at the Oval, and by his fine bowling helped the Players to win the match, sending down in the Gentlemen's second innings 15 overs for 44 runs and four wickets. Mr P. F. Warner was greatly impressed and predicted that Jeeves would be an England bowler in the near future. Within a month War had been declared. Jeeves was a right-handed bowler on the quick side of medium pace, and with an easy action came off the ground with plenty of spin. He was very popular among his brother players.

(*Wisden* 1917)

WEBBER, LIEUT. HENRY (South Lancashire Regiment), of Horley, Surrey, and a JP for the county, was killed in action on July 21, 1916, aged 68. He was in the Tonbridge School XI fifty years before, among his contemporaries being Mr J. W. Dale, and later played for Pembroke College, Oxford. He had been a member of the MCC since 1872. He made his first hundred in 1863 and as recently as August 6, 1904, when 56 years of age, made 209 not out for Horley v. Lowfield Heath, at Horley, in three hours after a full round of golf in the morning. His pluck and patriotism in insisting on being given a commission at his advanced age were much admired.

(*Wisden* 1917)

GEORGE TUBOW II, KING OF TONGA, the last of the independent kings in the Pacific, died April, 1918, aged 46. Very fond of cricket, gaining his love of the game while at school in Auckland. His subjects became so devoted to the game that it was necessary to prohibit it on six days of the week in order to avert famine, the plantations being entirely neglected for the cricket field.

(*Wisden* 1919)

ROUPELL, JOHN HARVEY TORRENS, who was born in Madras on July 15, 1845, died at Hurst, Berkshire, on May 15, 1920. He was educated at Harrow and Uppingham, and was in the latter XI in 1863. He was a tremendous hitter, a very fast round-armed bowler and a good field at long-on. In an innings of 97 for Trinity Hall v. Emmanuel College in June, 1865, he made clear hits for 10, 9, and 8, without any overthrows. 'The tenner travelled about 240 yards.'

(*Wisden* 1921)

RAE, EDWARD, who introduced the game into Russian Lapland, died at Birkenhead on June 26, 1923, aged 76.

(*Wisden* 1924)

DOUGLAS, JOHN WILLIAM HENRY TYLER, born at Clapton, Middlesex, on September 3, 1882, was drowned on December 19, 1930, in a collision which occurred in the Cattegat between the steamships *Oberon* and *Arcturus*. Together with his father, Mr J. H. Douglas, Mr Douglas, when the accident occurred, was a passenger on the *Oberon* returning to England from a business trip.

Johnny Douglas, as he was known in nearly every country where cricket is played, had a remarkable career. He was not only a fine cricketer but an even greater boxer and he attained some fame at Association football, appearing for the Corinthians and the Casuals and gaining an AFA international cap. While it was as a cricketer that he made his name a household word in so many parts of the world, he came to the front as a boxer when still at Felsted by his doings in the Public Schools' Championship. Later on, as he developed physically, he reached the highest class as a middle-weight and in 1905 won the Amateur Championship while in 1908 he carried off the Olympic Middle-Weight Championship by beating in a memorable encounter the Australian 'Snowy' Baker. So level were the men at the end of three rounds that neither judges nor referee could arrive at a decision and after an extra round the margin was of the narrowest.

Douglas learned his early cricket at Moulton Grammar School, Lincolnshire. He was in the Felsted XI in 1898, 1899, 1900 and 1901 and captain in the last of these years. It is curious, in view of the stolid batsman Douglas became, that when at Felsted he was coached by T. N. Perkins, a notable hitter in his Cambridge days. Douglas first appeared for Essex in 1901 – the year he left school – and had a most disheartening experience in his opening match being bowled in each innings by George Hirst's 'swerver' without making a run either time. He saw little of County Cricket during the next year or two and for some time afterwards was merely a useful all-round player. By 1908, however, he had thoroughly established his position in the Essex XI and three years later he showed he had about him the possibilities of an international player. He became captain of Essex in 1911 and continued to hold that post until the close of the season of 1928. In that summer of 1911, he enjoyed a great personal triumph in the Gentlemen and Players match at Lord's, scoring 72 and 22, not out, and taking seven wickets. This performance suggested he was the man for the big occasion and that he often proved in subsequent years. He had been out to New Zealand as a member of the MCC's team in the winter of 1906–07, distinguishing himself there with both bat and ball, and in the autumn of 1907 he had formed one of the sides Marylebone sent out to the United States and Canada.

Heavy responsibility was soon thrust upon his shoulders for P. F. Warner, who had been appointed captain of the team which went out to Australia in 1911–12, falling ill after the opening contest, the duties of leadership devolved upon Douglas. The first Test match was lost but, the side enjoying the services of those exceptionally fine bowlers, S. F. Barnes and F. R. Foster, the other four were won and so Douglas returned home with his reputation as a captain established. Strangely enough in the following summer – the season of the Triangular Tournament – when he might well have played for England in all six Tests, Douglas did not get a chance until the last match with Australia. For all that further honours soon fell to him as he was chosen to captain the MCC team in South Africa in 1913–14 when four Test games were won by England and the other drawn. After the War, in the course of which, getting a commission in the Bedfordshire Regiment, he reached the rank of Lieutenant-Colonel, Douglas was appointed captain of the MCC side that visited Australia in 1920–21 and lost all five Test matches. He played for England against Australia in the five Test contests of 1921 – in the first two as captain and in the remainder under the leadership of Tennyson. Finally he accompanied to Australia the team sent out under A. E. R. Gilligan in 1924–25 but played a very small part in that tour.

Possessed of exceptional defensive skill and inexhaustible patience, Douglas was a batsman very hard to dismiss. Sometimes, so intent was he upon keeping up his wicket, that he carried caution to excess and became tiresome to watch. Indeed, with his rather cramped style and limited number of strokes, he could never be described as an attractive player. Still there could be no question about his ability to face an awkward situation or about the soundness of his methods and, although so chary of investing his play with enterprise, he was able to hit with plenty of power on either side of the wicket. As a bowler he was a much more interesting figure. Distinctly above medium pace, he could keep at work for hours without losing either speed or length and to a new ball he 13 imparted, late in its flight, a very awkward swerve to leg. Always extremely fit, Douglas, even at the end of the hottest and longest day, scarcely knew what fatigue was and, if – strangely enough for a first-rate boxer – by no means quick on his feet in the cricket field, and therefore apt to miss the chance of making a catch, he never spared himself. As to his abilities as a captain on the field, opinions differed and he certainly was more brusque of manner than might be wished in a leader, but eloquent testimony in his favour was always forthcoming from players, professional as well as amateur, who had served under him on tours in other lands. To balance any lack of restraint in expressing his views about a blunder, he possessed that saving grace of humour which enjoyed tales against himself. How thoroughly he realised his limitations was shown by his remark 'An optimist is a man who, batting with Johnny Douglas, backs up for a run.' On one occasion Douglas batted an hour and a half for eight, not out, against Kent at Canterbury but, in so doing, he saved his side from defeat. His highest score was 210 not out for Essex against Derbyshire at Leyton in 1921. In company with A. E. Knight of Leicestershire, he put on for An England XI against the Australians at Blackpool in 1909 no fewer than 284 for the first wicket.

(Wisden 1931)

RANJITSINHJI, KUMAR SHRI. Almost the greatest tribute to the memory of HH The Jam Seheb of Nawanagar, whose sudden death at Delhi, on April 2, came as such a shock to the whole world of cricket, is the fact that everywhere he was referred to as 'Ranji'. It is scarcely necessary to add that this contraction of his name was used with true affection early in his career and remained to the end.

Born at Sarodar, Kathiawar, India, on September 10, 1872, Kumar Shri Ranjitsinhji came of ancient Rajput stock. He received his earliest lessons in cricket while at school at Rajkumar College, Rajkote, and when in 1888 he paid a visit to England he was, thanks to the coaching he had received from Mr Chester Macnaghten, a Cambridge man but not a 'Blue', a batsman of some skill but very unorthodox in his methods. Actually he played no cricket of any note in England until he went into residence at Trinity College, Cambridge where he secured a place in the college XI. Probably because he was an Indian he attracted a certain amount of attention but nobody who watched him playing for Cambridgeshire in 1892–93, and for Cambridge University when he was given his 'Blue' by F. S. Jackson in 1893, had the least idea that they were looking at a man who, in a few years, was to dazzle the world and bring about such an alteration in the methods of batting as definitely to mark a turning point in the history of the game. It is not too much to say that by his extraordinary skill Ranjitsinhji revolutionised cricket, the effects of his wonderful play on the leg-side being seen day after day down to the present time.

If a little crude and most certainly unreliable at the outset, Ranjitsinhji was blessed with a most versatile brain and the capacity for application which in course of time made him one of the most brilliant batsmen ever seen. Quite individual and distinctive in style, he possessed exceptional keenness of eye, besides such power and flexibility of wrist, that on a fast wicket he could do almost anything in the way of scoring. Admitting the use of the word in connection with cricket, genius could with the greatest truth be applied to him. Thanks to his special gifts he could – and did – take the good length ball off the middle-stump and glance it to leg with a measure of certainty no one else has ever equalled or even approached. In this way he was no safe model for any player of average skill, for the attempt to bring off many of his strokes must have been fatal to most people.

Ranjitsinhji did not attain to this pitch of perfection without much hard work. For two or three seasons before he got his 'Blue' he put in hours of practice at the nets with Lockwood, Richardson, J. T. Hearne and Tom Hayward bowling at him. The first two, then almost at their zenith in regard to pace and accuracy, had definite instructions from him always to try and bowl at their fastest when he was having practice, and the value of this intensive training was seen a few years later when he blossomed forth as a batsman able to bring off the most daring strokes. To begin with he was not a player at all on soft wickets, but he steadily increased his ability to make runs under adverse conditions and put together some remarkable innings on bowlers' pitches. Primarily, however, he was a fast-wicket batsman because, for the successful exploitation of his own particular strokes, hard turf was essential. When he first came out he appeared to lack the strength necessary for driving, making nearly all his runs behind or square with the wicket, and mainly on the leg-side. But before long he employed the drive a lot and invested that stroke with plenty of power. In many of his displays he gave full proof that he could score with readiness in front of the wicket, but by those who watched him throughout his great days he will be remembered best for the extraordinary skill with which he glanced the ball to leg.

In the only university match in which he took part he did nothing of any consequence, but in that season at Cambridge he played some good innings and against the Australians scored 58 and not out 37 in splendid style. I was present at that match and never forgot the impression he created on my mind. I knew that I was watching an accomplished batsman, but little thought that the lithe, supple figure then playing such bowlers as George Giffen, C. T. B. Turner and

Hugh Trumble, to mention nothing of Bob McLeod, Harry Trott and Billy Bruce, with consummate ease and confidence was to become and to remain from 1895 until 1912 – with two breaks of four years each – the most talked-of man in cricket.

Deciding to stay in England after leaving Cambridge, Ranjitsinhji duly qualified for Sussex, and in 1895 commenced a memorable association with that county which continued unbroken up to 1904. No happier augury for his future success could have occurred than when on the occasion of his first appearance for Sussex, against the MCC at Lord's, he scored 77 not out and 150. That summer he obtained 1,775 runs and averaged nearly 50. A year later this performance was completely eclipsed. His average went up to nearly 58 and he registered no fewer than 2,780 runs. This was the highest aggregate obtained by any one up to that date and, what was of greatest importance, bigger than that of W. G. Grace – 2,739 in 1871 – which had stood as the record for a quarter of a century. The seasons of 1901 and 1904 also brought Ranjitsinhji aggregates of over 2,000 runs, while in 1899 and 1900 he exceeded 3,000, his totals respectively for those years being 3,159 and 3,065. In 1900 he had the remarkable average of 87. Altogether in the course of his career he scored 24,567 runs with an average of 45, and played 72 three-figure innings – ten during the summer of 1896. On fourteen occasions he reached 200, obtaining all these scores for Sussex and five of them in 1900. In that year he twice obtained three hundreds in succession – 127 against Gloucestershire, 222 against Somerset, and 215 not out against Cambridge University and, later in the season, his scores were 103 against Surrey, 202 against Middlesex, and 109 against Gloucestershire. It must be mentioned too that in 1896 he accomplished the feat of making three consecutive hundreds, getting 100 and 125 not out against Yorkshire immediately following 165 against

Lancashire. In the match with Yorkshire he went in on the second evening, but had not scored at the drawing of stumps, so that he really made two separate hundreds on the same day.

Among the many big partnerships in which he was concerned were two of over 300; he and W. Newham scored 344 for the seventh wicket in the Sussex and Essex match of 1902, and 325 for the second wicket came with George Brann in the game between Sussex and Surrey in 1899. Taunton, always one of his favourite grounds, was in 1901 the scene of his highest individual score – 285 not out against Somerset. In county cricket probably his most masterly display was that at Hove in 1900 when against Middlesex he got 202 in three hours. The pitch helped the bowlers considerably, but Ranjitsinhji triumphed over all the difficulties and actually hit thirty-five fours. He was, however, always insistent that the best innings he played on a hard wicket was his 234 not out at Hastings in 1902 when in the match between Sussex and Surrey 1,427 runs were scored and only 21 wickets went down. Richardson and Lockwood were among the Surrey bowlers, but Ranjitsinhji batted so superbly that he made both of them look just ordinary. His driving was wonderful. Some years afterwards he said to me, apropos of this innings and without any trace of boasting in his remarks, 'I think I could have stayed there for ever, for the ball looked as big as a balloon the whole time I was in.' By a sad coincidence, Hastings was the ground on which in 1920 he played in his last match in England – Sussex v. Northamptonshire. He had then grown very stout and suffered from the grave disability of having lost one of his eyes, through an accident when out shooting. I saw both these matches and well remember the feeling of sorrow which came over me when I realised the inevitable change which the passage of years had wrought in his wonderful powers of execution. It is of interest to know, however, that his one idea in coming back and playing cricket after the War was prompted by his desire to write another book on cricket, with special emphasis on the art of batting with only one eye. As he said at the time, he could deal with good-length balls almost as well as formerly, but the long-hop or half-volley caused him real trouble in properly focussing his sight.

Ranjitsinhji was captain of Sussex for five years – 1899 to 1903. Returning to India after the summer of 1904 he did not play again until 1908 when he turned out and obtained over 1,100 runs. There came a similar interval after that, and in 1912 returning once more to first-class cricket, he made more than 1,100 runs.

Taking part in fourteen Test matches – five in Australia – he scored in the course of those games 989 runs with an average of nearly 45. When, in the winter of 1897–98, he formed one of A. E. Stoddart's second team to Australia, he played an innings of 175 at Sydney but as an England cricketer his great triumph was that at Manchester in 1896 when he scored 154 not out in superb style, being so completely master of the Australian bowling that, could he have got anybody to stay with him, he might have saved England from defeat. As it was, the Australians wanted only 125 to win, but Ranjitsinhji's splendid batting was followed by some of the most magnificent bowling ever seen, on the part of Tom Richardson, and seven wickets went down before the runs were obtained, Richardson being on for three hours without sending down one really loose ball.

While his general record in Test matches against Australia came out quite well, Ranjitsinhji finished his career in those games ingloriously in 1902 when, curiously enough, he had as his companion in misfortune C. B. Fry. Here were two of the greatest batsmen in the world, but a more deplorable failure than that of both could not well be imagined. Ranjitsinhji, in the course of

19

three matches, scored 13, 0, 2, and 0, and Fry 0, 0, 1, and 4. Still, those particular contests furnished the only serious blot on a wonderful career. Ranjitsinhji figured prominently in Gentlemen v. Players matches. He made his first appearance in 1893 and his last in 1912, his score of 121 at Lord's in 1904 being his best.

In 1897 he wrote the *Jubilee Book of Cricket* and two years later he took a team to America.

So has passed a great character in the history of the game. We may never see his like again, for he burst on the cricket horizon at the start of what has been described as its most brilliant era, when there existed scope for introducing new ideas and methods.

Ranjitsinhji was the embodiment of all that a cricketer should be – generous in defeat, modest in success and genuinely enthusiastic regarding the achievements of either colleagues or opponents.

(*Wisden* 1934)

MILLAR, CHARLES CHRISTIAN HOYER, founder and for fifty-five years president of Rosslyn Park Rugby football club, who died on November 22, 1942, aged 81, deserved mention in *Wisden* for a very special and unique reason. He undertook on his own initiative to 'weed' Lord's turf, and Sir Francis Lacey, secretary of MCC, signed a deed of appointment making him 'Honorary Weedkiller to GHQ Cricket'. From 1919 to 1931 he kept up his task, being particularly busy on summer evenings after stumps were drawn, and his zeal often received comment from pressmen walking to the exit when their duties were done. Mr Millar, according to his own reckoning, accounted for 624,000 'victims', having spent 956 hours in his war against plantains and other 'unwanted vegetation'.

(*Wisden* 1943)

MACLAREN, ARCHIBALD CAMPBELL, very prominent in cricket during a long career lasting altogether from 1887 to 1923, died on November 17, 1944, when nearly 73 years of age. An immaculate batsman possessing the grand manner, he would have gained still higher renown on the playing field but for periods of poor health and the calls of business. Expert knowledge, obtained by careful study of every intricacy of the game, besides experience in leading his school, his county, the Gentlemen and England, might have made him supreme as captain, but he lacked the buoyant optimistic temperament so necessary for complete success in cricket and was easily upset by disagreement with selectors in being given players whom he did not consider suitable to the occasion.

To satisfy his own exacting ideas of perfect play and leadership, as described in his book *Cricket Old and New*, he required the position of dictator in order to pick his own XI and control them with expectation of ready response to his every word or gesture. Unfortunately for MacLaren, such idealistic conditions were never forthcoming on the big occasion, but the responsibility for this rested partly with him more than once, when he was one of the selectors. Facts bear this out, as will be seen; but in batting he accomplished much, and will remain a magnificent figure in the eyes of all who saw him making runs.

He will always be remembered for his 424 for Lancashire against Somerset at Taunton in 1895, a first-class score that stood unbeaten for nearly thirty years and has been exceeded only by Don Bradman, who now holds the record with 452 not out, and W. H. Ponsford in Australia. For choice as a Test captain he remains unrivalled, having in the course of eleven years led England in twenty-two matches, and his thirty-five appearances against Australia have been surpassed only by Hobbs and Rhodes during far longer periods. Often unfortunate when commander in these big events, he never led England to victory in a rubber, but showed his exceptional knowledge of the game when, having asserted that he could pick a side capable of beating the all-conquering Australian team of 1921, he fulfilled his prophecy by selecting and captaining eleven amateurs, who, at Eastbourne at the end of August, gained a victory by 28 runs after being 130 behind on the first innings. In that climax to his career in England he retained his superb figure, though white hair suggested more age than the approach of his fiftieth birthday. He finished his intimate association with first-class cricket by acting as manager to S. B. Joel's team that toured South Africa in 1924-25.

Son of Mr James MacLaren, for many years Hon. Treasurer of Lancashire CC, Archie MacLaren was born on December 1, 1871, at Manchester, and began his important cricket life auspiciously when only 15 years of age by scoring 55 and 67 for Harrow against Eton in 1887. He finished four years in the XI as captain, and with 76 in a total of 133 off the Eton bowlers at Lord's, showed such form that a month later he appeared in County Cricket, and in his first match for Lancashire played a fine innings of 108 against Sussex at Hove.

His obvious powers took some time to ripen, but within a few years he reached the front rank of batsmen. Possessed of great resource, he could, according to circumstances, play a cautious or a brilliant game that made him splendid to watch from the ringside. Standing erect with bat raised well behind him, he was ready to receive any kind of delivery and would force the ball away with every sort of powerful stroke.

Captain of Lancashire from 1894 to 1896, and again from 1899 to 1907, he reasserted himself in 1921 as described, and in the winter of 1922-23, at the age of 51, when leading an MCC side in New Zealand, he scored 200 not out at Wellington in a representative match. Besides his record 424, he three times exceeded 200 for his county, 226 at Canterbury against Kent in 1896, next year 244 in the same fixture, and 204 at Liverpool against Gloucester in 1903. From 1893 to 1909 he frequently appeared for Gentlemen against Players, making 728 runs in these games with an average of 45; in 1903, when he and C. B. Fry added 309 in three hours for the third wicket without being separated, he scored 168.

Eight times in England and once in Australia he obtained over 1,000 runs in a season, his largest aggregate being 1,886 (average 42) in the summer of 1903. He enjoyed pronounced success on the Sydney ground, where in the winter of 1897–98 against New South Wales he scored 142 and 100 in one match, 109 and 50 not out a month later against Australia, 61 and 140 in another match with New South Wales, and 65 in the last Test. He also got 124 against Australia at Adelaide and 181 at Brisbane, altogether six centuries on that tour, in which he made 1,037 runs, average 54.57, in first-class matches. No wonder that MacLaren is still talked of in Australia, and especially at Sydney, for his wonderful batting as an object lesson for everyone.

In Test matches between England and Australia he made 1,931 runs, four times reaching three figures and averaging nearly 34. Twice in the '90s he toured Australia with teams led by A. E. Stoddart, and in the winter of 1901–02 he himself took out a side; but in Test matches this team, like the second captained by Stoddart, suffered four defeats and gained only one victory. In three home seasons – 1899, 1902 and 1909 – England, captained by him, won only two of fourteen engagements and lost each rubber. MacLaren visited America with K. S. Ranjitsinhji's team in 1899, and the Argentine in 1911–12 with the MCC side led by Lord Hawke, and he also played in India.

He astonished everyone by taking S. F. Barnes, of small experience in first-class cricket, on the 1901–02 tour in Australia. Yet he could not keep that wonderful bowler in the Lancashire county XI, and in 1909 he failed to persuade his county colleague, Walter Brearley, then the best of our fast bowlers, to accept a last-moment invitation to play for England at Lord's.

Opinions differ as to the ability of MacLaren as a captain. Everyone agrees that he held strong views and was loath to depart from them even if his leadership actually suffered. In fact, it appeared more than once that he pursued ways that showed up some curious decision of selection committees in carrying out their duties.

Undoubtedly he found occasional brilliant inspirations, born of his exceptional knowledge of cricket, but he committed some blunders difficult to understand in a man of his experience. A notable illustration of his erratic disposition occurred at the Oval in the Test match of 1909. To begin with, having the final word in the composition of the XI, he decided, despite fine weather and a hard wicket, that England should take the field without a good fast bowler, John Sharp, of Lancashire, being preferred to Buckenham, of Essex. Then, with the score 9 and one man out, he took Sidney Barnes off in favour of Sharp, mainly a batsman, and kept D. W. Carr, a googly bowler, aged 37, on at one end for an hour and a half, an action for which it would have been difficult to excuse anybody. That was the match in which Warren Bardsley made 136 and 130.

Another lapse from wisdom was at Old Trafford in 1902, when he sent to deep square leg Fred Tate, always a short slip: and that historic dropped catch brought about England's defeat in a match upon which the rubber depended – only victory in that engagement could have prevented the honours going to Australia. Yet such was

his knowledge of the game that at Leeds in 1904 he gave Yorkshire first innings, and Lancashire, by avoiding defeat in George Hirst's benefit match, went through the season unbeaten and were champions for the only time under MacLaren's captaincy.

An incident in which MacLaren took strong action was of a kind without precedent or repetition, so far as known, and it aroused severe criticism. In July 1907 at Lord's on the second day the paying public were admitted although saturated turf showed no sign of drying and any cricket was extremely unlikely. Yet the stumps were set, and when pulled up at quarter to five some of the crowd, after demonstrating in front of the pavilion, walked across the pitch. After prolonged discussion between the captains – Gregor MacGregor led Middlesex – and umpires, this statement was handed to the Press by A. C. MacLaren himself: 'Owing to the pitch having been deliberately torn up by the public, I, as captain of the Lancashire XI, cannot see any way to continue the game, the groundsman bearing me out that the wicket could not be again put right. – A. C. MacLaren.' As described in the 1908 *Wisden*, the match was accordingly abandoned. Rolled next morning for the regulation ten minutes, the pitch showed little trace of the damage.

Naturally such a cricketer received many tributes to his ability. In January 1896 the Lancashire club elected him a life member and presented him with a gold watch and chain in recognition of his record score and of three successive hundreds hit in the course of eight days at the end of August that same season – 152 at Old Trafford against Nottinghamshire, 108 at Lord's against Middlesex, and 135 at Leicester. Ten years later Lancashire made him a special presentation. In September 1921 he accepted an appointment to coach young players of the county, but an injured knee compelled his resignation early in the 1923 season.

GANDAR-DOWER, KENNETH CECIL, was lost at sea through Japanese action in February, 1944, at the age of 36. He played for Harrow against Winchester in 1927, but not in the Eton match. At Cambridge he did well in the Freshmen's match and was a Crusader, but his time was mainly given up to tennis, at which he captained the University team. One of the most versatile players of games of any period, he was amateur squash champion in 1938, won amateur championships at fives, and played lawn tennis for Great Britain. In all, he represented Cambridge at six forms of sport: tennis, lawn tennis, Rugby fives, Eton fives, squash racquets and billiards. In fact, time hardly sufficed for their rival calls. He probably created a record when he played simultaneously in the Freshmen's match and Freshmen's tournament, with the connivance of the tennis but not the cricket authorities; he disappeared to play off a round during the early part of his side's innings, with relays of cyclist friends to keep him informed as to the fall of wickets! He flew a private aeroplane to India. In spite of other demands he continued to find time for cricket, making some ten appearances for the Frogs each season almost to the outbreak of war, and got many runs and wickets.

Famous as a big game shot, and extensive traveller, he introduced a team of cheetahs from Kenya jungle to London and on greyhound tracks they set up speed records. A writer of articles and books, he acted as a War Correspondent in various theatres of operations up to the time of his death.

(*Wisden* 1946)

HM KING GEORGE VI, died at Sandringham on February 6, 1952. He was Patron of the Marylebone, Surrey and Lancashire clubs. When Prince Albert he performed the hat-trick on the private ground on the slopes below Windsor Castle, where the sons and grandsons of Edward VII used to play regularly. A left-handed batsman and bowler, the King bowled King Edward VII, King George V and the present Duke of Windsor in three consecutive balls, thus proving himself the best Royal cricketer since Frederick, Prince of Wales, in 1751, took a keen interest in the game. The ball is now mounted in the mess-room of the Royal Naval College, Dartmouth. King George VI, like his father, often went to Lord's when Commonwealth teams were playing there, and invariably the players and umpires were presented to His Majesty in front of the pavilion. He entertained the 1948 Australian team at Balmoral, and in his 1949 New Year's Honours Donald Bradman, the captain, received a Knighthood.

(*Wisden* 1953)

FERGUSON, WILLIAM HENRY, who died at Bath on September 22, 1957, aged 77, was the best-known cricket scorer in the world. For fifty-two years, from the time he first visited England with Joe Darling's Australian side of 1905, he acted as scorer and baggage-master for England, South Africa, West Indies, New Zealand and, naturally, Australia, in no fewer than forty-three tours. In all that time his boast was that he never lost a bag. 'Fergie', as he was affectionately known in the cricket world, scored in no fewer than 208 Test matches in every country where big cricket is played. He liked to relate how he first took up the job. The office in Sydney, his birthplace, where he was employed as a clerk, overlooked the harbour and he often felt the urge to travel. So in 1905 he 'thought up a nice toothache', went to see his dentist, M. A. Noble, the Test batsman, and brought up the question of scoring. Amused at the ingenious method of approach, Noble put forward 'Fergie's' name to the authorities, with the result that this short, slightly-built man began his travels which totalled well over half a million miles. His salary for the 1905 tour was £2 per week, from which he defrayed his expenses, and he paid his own passage.

For all his long connection with it, 'Fergie' never took much active part in the game, but figures, for which he always had a passion, fascinated him, and he loved to travel. Besides actual scoring, he kept diagrams of every stroke played, with their value, by every batsman in the matches in which he was concerned, and could account for every ball bowled – and who fielded it. Touring captains, including D. G. Bradman and D. R. Jardine, employed his charts to study the strength and weaknesses of opposing batsmen.

When in England with the Australian team of 1948, 'Fergie' was presented to King George VI. That summer Bradman scored 2,428 runs. Said the King: 'Mr Ferguson, do you use an adding-machine when the Don is in?'

'Fergie', who received the British Empire Medal in 1951 for his services to cricket, emerged from two years' retirement to score for the West Indies last summer. A fall at an hotel in August prevented him from finishing the tour, and he spent some time in hospital, returning home only two days before his death. His autobiography, titled *Mr Cricket*, was published in May, 1957.

(*Wisden* 1958)

FILLISTON, JOSEPH W., who died in hospital on October 25, 1964, aged 102, five days after being knocked down by a motor-scooter, acted as umpire to the BBC Cricket Club for many years. 'Old Joe' stood in the Old England v. Lord's Taverners match at Lord's when over 100. In his younger days he played cricket with Dr W. G. Grace and he helped Gentlemen of Kent defeat the Philadelphians by six wickets at Town Malling in 1889. He also played as a professional in the Staffordshire League. He liked to tell of the occasion when he gave 'W. G.' out leg-before in a London County game at the Crystal Palace. The Doctor, he said, refused to leave the crease and, as nobody had the courage to contradict him, he continued his innings.

(*Wisden* 1965)

SIR FRANK WORRELL
BORN IN BARBADOS, AUGUST 1, 1924
DIED IN JAMAICA, MARCH 13, 1967
KNIGHTED FOR HIS SERVICES TO CRICKET, 1964
by Sir Learie Constantine

Sir Frank Worrell once wrote that the island of Barbados, his birthplace, lacked a hero. As usual, he was under-playing himself. Frank Maglinne Worrell was the first hero of the new nation of Barbados and anyone who doubted that had only to be in the island when his body was brought home in mid March of 1967.

Or in Westminster Abbey when West Indians of all backgrounds and shades of opinion paid their last respects to a man who had done more than any other of their countrymen to bind together the new nations of the Caribbean and establish a reputation for fair play throughout the world. Never before had a cricketer been honoured with a memorial service in Westminster Abbey.

Sir Frank was a man of strong convictions, a brave man and it goes without saying, a great cricketer. Though he made his name as a player his greatest contribution was to destroy for ever the myth that a coloured cricketer was not fit to lead a team. Once

29

appointed, he ended the cliques and rivalries between the players of various islands to weld together a team which in the space of five years became the champions of the world.

He was a man of true political sense and feeling, a federalist who surely would have made even greater contributions to the history of the West Indies had he not died so tragically in hospital of leukaemia at the early age of 42, a month after returning from India.

People in England can have little idea of the problems of West Indian cricket. It is not a question of a few countries bordering each other coming together in a joint team. Jamaica is 1,296 flying miles from Barbados, and Georgetown in Guyana 462 miles from Bridgetown in Barbados.

Before that wonderful tour of Australia in 1960–61, Barbadians would tend to stick together and so would the Trinidadians, Jamaicans and Guyanans. Worrell cut across all that. Soon there were no groups. Just one team.

He told his batsmen to walk if they were given out. When Gary Sobers appeared to show his dissent with a decision, he reprimanded him. After that, everyone walked as soon as the umpire's finger went up.

So when half a million Australians lined the streets of Melbourne in their ticker tape farewell to Worrell and his men, they were not only paying a final tribute to the team's great achievements, they were recognising the capacity and potential of equals both on and off the turf.

Sir Frank started life in Barbados, worked and lived in Trinidad and died in Jamaica after doing much useful work at the University of the West Indies there. He incurred enmity by leaving his birthplace but he did not care much for insularity, cant and humbug.

30   He saw the many diverse elements of the West Indies as a whole,

a common culture and outlook separated only by the Caribbean Sea. This is why he upset certain people in Barbados when he wrote to a newspaper there criticising the island for having the cheek to challenge the rest of the world to celebrate independence.

Worrell was strongly criticised for this action, bitterly in fact in some quarters. But being attacked did not worry him. He always had the courage to say what he felt about every issue he thought vital to the well-being of the islands.

Sadly, the news that he was dying came through as Barbados played the Rest of the World XI. But Worrell held no rancour against his homeland. He had bought a piece of land there and had intended to retire there eventually.

This willingness to speak out often got him into trouble, even at school. Cricket had come naturally to him as it does to most youngsters in the West Indies, particularly Barbados. More so with him because he was born in a house only a few yards away from the Empire cricket ground. He and his friends used to set up stumps on the outfield and play nearly all day in the holidays.

At Combermere School he fell foul of a master who accused him of hogging the crease and not letting his colleagues bat.

He was to write later: 'I was unfortunate enough to have been under an endemic psychological and mental strain throughout my school days. So much so that by the time I reached the fourth form I was suffering from a persecution complex.

'These were the days when child psychology was not a subject demanded of applicants to teachers' posts. Indeed, the majority of masters did not have the experience of raising families of their own. There was no allowance for the original point of view.'

Worrell was a pupil who always had an original point of view. Also, as it was becoming clear at this time, he was a cricketer with an original talent. He soon made the Barbados team and records began to flow from his bat as he moved up the order from number eleven (yes, that is where he began his career!).

He shared a partnership of 502 with John Goddard in 1943–44 and an unfinished 574 with Clyde Walcott in 1945–46. Typically he dismissed both. 'The conditions were loaded in our favour,' he said. 'I wasn't all that delighted about it.'

In 1947 he tired of living in Barbados. His mother had moved to New York and his father was away at sea most of the time so he moved to Jamaica. English people will be surprised to learn that many of Worrell's fellow Bajans have never forgiven him for this 'betrayal'. When will they ever learn?

He established an international reputation against the 1947–48 England touring side and at the end of that tour took the step that made him a batsman for all seasons and all wickets. He signed as professional for the Central Lancashire League side Radcliffe for a fee of £500 a year.

It was a good year to enter League cricket. The Central Lancashire League was a cricket academy and the young, talented player was bound to improve by the experience. Playing in neighbouring clubs were Bill Alley, Jock Livingston, Ray Lindwall, Cecil Pepper, Clyde Walcott, Everton Weekes, Vinoo Mankad and Dattu Phadkar.

I have always held that League cricket makes a cricketer, not only as a player but as a man. There is much to learn in the field of human relations from the kind, friendly and warm people of the North of England. Frank brought his fiancée, Velda, over and their marriage was another settling influence on him.

Worrell was not just living for the present – as I regret is the case with some of our cricketers – but he was thinking of the future. He took a course at Manchester University and qualified in economics, his chosen subject.

The flag on Radcliffe Town Hall was at half mast on the day of his death. He married his wife, Velda, at Radcliffe, and their daughter was born there. Such was the esteem in which he was held by Radcliffe that in 1964 a street near the cricket ground was named Worrell Close.

The 1950 tour of England was a triumph for him and he topped the Test batting averages with 539 runs at an average of 89.83. His best Test score of 261 was made in this season, at Trent Bridge.

Norman Yardley, the England captain of the time, told me it was impossible to set a field to him. Place the fieldsmen straight and he beat them on the wide. Place them wide and he would beat them straight.

I am not one for averages myself. I am more concerned with how a batsman made his runs and not what his average was at the end of the series. Sir Neville Cardus has written of Sir Frank that he never made a crude or an ungrammatical stroke. I agree with that. Worrell was poetry.

While Walcott bludgeoned the bowlers and Weekes dominated them, the stylist Worrell waved them away. There was none of the savage aggression of a Sobers in his batting. He was the artist. All three 'Ws' were geniuses but Worrell was my favourite because he had more style and elegance. He had all the strokes and the time and capacity to use them without offence to the eye, without ever being hurried.

He was never seen playing across the line. That is why he never hooked. Players and Pressmen agreed that even when he ducked beneath a bouncer, he did so with a lack of panic and great dignity. And remember he had Lindwall and Miller to contend with!

The tour to Australia in 1951–52 was not such a success as the 1950 tour of England. Worrell himself said this was because there were too many factions in the side and John Goddard, previously showered with advice, was not helped this time by the seniors.

When Worrell took over the captaincy nine years later, he was to heed the lessons of this dismal tour. The return series in the West Indies in 1955 was again a disappointment for Worrell; he scored only 206 runs. The 1957 tour of England was a further let down. Clearly the West Indies authorities had to change their policy of always appointing a white man to captain the side.

The break was made in 1960 when Worrell, the only candidate with the outstanding qualities to do this gigantic repair job, was asked to lead the side in Australia. Everyone knows the story of that tour and how much it did to restore the good name of cricket after the 'bumper' rows, 'slow over rates' disputes and other ills which had been afflicting the international game.

Back in Jamaica, Worrell was acclaimed and rightly so. He was appointed Warden of the University College of the West Indies and also a Senator in Parliament.

The Indians were the next tourists to the West Indies and it was typical of the man that when their captain, Nari Contractor, was seriously injured by a blow on the head, Worrell was one of the donors of blood which saved his life.

It was not generally known that Worrell, the thirteenth West Indies captain, was a superstitious man. During the 1951 tour of Australia he was bowled first ball by Geoff Noblet. Determined to make a fresh start in the second innings, he changed every stitch of clothing, fitting himself out in a completely new gear and walked to the wicket hoping that by discarding his old clothes he would change his luck. Not a bit of it! He was out for another first baller!

As he came in, crestfallen, Clyde Walcott, the next batsman, said with a laugh: 'Why do I have to face a hat-trick every time I follow you?'

His finest hours in England came in 1963 when he led the West Indies to more glory. By this time he had slowed up in the field and his figure was well in excess of Miss World proportions. He was 38 (age I mean) and no longer the player he had been. He was a tired man and often told me so.

But his influence over the side as captain was such that it was unthinkable to rest him in any of the Tests. He bowled a few shrewd medium pacers with his deceptively easy delivery and when the crisis was on in the Lord's Test, the greatest Test of all times as it was called by the critics, he helped Butcher to add 110 on the Saturday afternoon. The following Monday morning the second innings collapsed.

Asked if Worrell was worried about this, another player replied: 'No, he is asleep.' Sir Frank had this ability to drop off at any time, particularly when there was a batting collapse. After his death, I wondered whether this had something to do with his illness which was obviously affecting him at this time, though no one knew that he was not a fit man.

As Wes Hall prepared for the final over which could have won or lost the Lord's Test, Worrell went to him with some advice. What was he saying? Bounce them? Bowl 'em straight? No, none of the obvious things. Sir Frank said calmly: 'Make sure you don't give it to them by bowling no balls.' Worrell was the calmest man at Lord's that day and trust him to think of a highly pertinent point which Hall, in his excitement, may have overlooked!

He announced his retirement at the end of this tour which was a triumph of leadership, technical skill and adaptability. The following year Her Majesty the Queen knighted this complete Cricketer, Philosopher and Captain. It was a fitting end to an unforgettable career but there was one more job for him to do – manage the West Indies side against the 1965 Australian tourists. 35

He had groomed Sobers well for the captaincy and theirs was an unbeatable partnership. At last the West Indies were the undisputed champions in their truly national sport.

Throughout his life, Sir Frank never lost his sense of humour or his sense of dignity. Some nasty things were said and written during that 1965 tour but Sir Frank was ever the diplomat. He lost no friends, made no enemies yet won more respect. He would always come up with a smile and a loud laugh. West Indians really laugh their laughs. And Sir Frank laughed louder than most of us.

He was a happy man, a good man and a great man. The really tragic thing about his death at the age of 42 was that it cut him off from life when he still had plenty to offer the islands he loved. He was only at the beginning. Or was it that the opportunity came to him a bit too late?

(Wisden 1968)

WILFRED RHODES
BORN AT KIRKHEATON, WEST RIDING, OCTOBER, 29, 1877
DIED NEAR HIS HOME IN DORSET, JULY 8, 1973
HE HAD BEEN BLIND SINCE 1952
by Sir Neville Cardus

Wilfred Rhodes was Yorkshire cricket personified in the great period of the county's domination, shrewd, dour, but quick to seize opportunity. For Yorkshire he scored more than 30,000 runs, averaging 30 an innings: for Yorkshire he took 3,608 wickets at 16 runs each. When he was not playing for Yorkshire, in his spare time, so to say, he played for England and amassed 2,000 runs, average 30, and took 127 wickets, at the cost of 26.96 apiece. In his first Test match he was last in the batting order, and at Sydney in the 1903–04 rubber he took part in the most persistent and prolific Test match last-wicket partnership to this day; he helped R. E. Foster to add 130 for the tenth wicket, his share 40 not out. Eight years afterwards he went in first for England at Melbourne, and against Australia he was the partner of Hobbs in the record first-wicket stand of 323.

His career is already legendary; it does indeed read like a fairy tale. He was not 21 years old when he first bowled for Yorkshire in a match against MCC at Lord's. In the first innings he accounted for Trott and Chatterton; in the second for Trott, Chatterton, C. P. Foley, and the Hon. J. R. Tufton – six wickets for 63, a modest beginning, true. But at the season's end he had established himself as the greatest slow left-hand bowler in England with 154 wickets, average 14.60.

During the period in which Rhodes and Hobbs opened every England innings by prescriptive right, Rhodes put aside his bowling. In the Australian rubber of 1911–12 he contributed only 18 overs. But then the War came, reducing the Yorkshire attack. In 1919 Yorkshire needed again the spin and flight of Rhodes, so he picked up his bowling arts exactly where years before he had laid them down, picked them up as though he had not lost touch for a moment. He headed the bowling averages of 1919, 164 wickets, average 14.42 in 1,048 overs. He was nearly 42 by the calendar. In 1902 he had gone in last for England at Kennington Oval when 15 runs were wanted to beat Australia; George Hirst, with whom he always opened Yorkshire's attack, was holding the wicket at the other end. England won by one wicket.

Twenty-four years afterwards, Rhodes in his forty-ninth year was recalled to the England XI and was one of the main causes of Australia's defeat and England's emergence from years in the wilderness. On this, his last appearance for England, Rhodes took the wickets of Woodfull, Ponsford, Richardson (twice), Collins, and Bardsley for 79 runs. He had probably lost by then much of his old quick vitally fingered spin: but as he explained to me: 'If batsmen thinks as I'm spinnin' them, then I am' – a remark metaphysical, maybe, but to the point. At Sydney, in December, 1903, on the shirt-fronted polished Bulli soil pitches of that distant halcyon day of batsmen, Australia scored 485, and the might of Australia's champions commanded the crease – Trumper, Hill, Duff, Armstrong, Gregory. Rhodes bowled 48 overs for 94 runs, five wickets. It was on this occasion that Trumper, most brilliant of all batsmen, alive or dead, made his famous remark to Rhodes – 'for God's sake, Wilfred, give me a minute's rest.'

Rhodes could not turn the ball on the Australian grounds of half a century ago. He prevailed by length, variations of flight, but chiefly by unceasing accuracy of pitch, always demanding close attention from the batsman, the curving arc through the air, the ball dropping on the same spot over by over, yet not on quite the same spot, each over in collusion with the rest, every ball a decoy, some balls apparently guileless, some artfully masked – and one of them, sooner or later, the master ball. He was economical in action, a few short strides, then a beautifully balanced sideways swing of the body, the arm loose and making a lovely arch. He could go on for hours; the rhythm of his action was in its easy rotation, hypnotic, lulling his victims to the tranced state in which he could work his will, make them perform strokes contrary to their reason and intention. Batsmen of Rhodes's heyday frequently succumbed to his bait for a catch in the deep field. David Denton had safe hands at long-on; and the score-sheets of the period repeated day by day the rubric – 'c Denton b Rhodes'. In rainy weather, 'c Tunnicliffe b Rhodes' was familiar proof that Wilfred was at work on a 'sticky' pitch, for Tunnicliffe was the best slip fielder of the century, a long giant with a reach into infinity.

Rhodes really was a slow bowler, not quick and low flight to the pitch, after Lock's manner. At the end of his career he proudly maintained that 'Ah were never hooked and Ah were never cut,' a pardonable exaggeration considering the proportion of truth in it. Rhodes seldom pitched short. 'Best ball on a "sticky" pitch is a spinnin' half-volley,' such was his doctrine. And he bowled to his field with the precision of high mathematics. Ernest Tyldesley once told me that he often had no alternative but to play at least three balls an over, on a batsman's wicket, straight to mid-off, an inch off the spot where Rhodes had planted mid-off.

Rhodes made himself into a batsman by practice and hard thinking. He was one of the first batsmen to adopt the full-fronted stance, left shoulder pointing to forward leg. But it is a mistake to suppose that his batting was perpetually dour and parsimonious in strokeplay. In the Test match against the Australians at Lord's in 1912, England had first innings on a rain-damaged pitch. *Wisden* relates that Rhodes, with Hobbs as company, 'so monopolised the hitting that his share of 77 runs amounted to 52.' On the whole and naturally enough, Rhodes distrusted the romantic gesture. One day in conversation with him, I deplored the absence in modern cricket of the cut. 'But it were never a business stroke,' he maintained.

While he was actively engaged in the game he was not a man given to affability. He was known as a 'natterer' on the field; and to natter in the North of England means to talk naggingly, mostly to oneself, with the intention of being overheard. At Old Trafford in the '30s Lancashire reached a total of 500 against Yorkshire. The Lancashire captain, Leonard Green, was about to take the bowling of Rhodes when the score was 499. Green was sure in his mind that a total of 500 would never again, or not for decades, be achieved by Lancashire against Yorkshire. He therefore determined that come what may he would himself score the 500th run. So he blocked a ball from Rhodes, then ran like the wind. The ball was picked up by Emmott Robinson at silly-point, and hurled to the bowler's end, where it struck Rhodes on the wrist even as Green got home by the skin of his teeth. And in all the scurry and excitement Wilfred was heard to mutter, while he retrieved Robinson's violent throw, 'There's somebody runnin' up and down this wicket. Ah don't know who it is, but there's somebody runnin' up and down this wicket.'

He was a great player, one of the greatest in cricket's history, not only for his all-round performances denoted by the statisticians: nearly 40,000 runs scored in 37 seasons and 4,184 wickets taken. He was great because his cricket was redolent and representative of Yorkshire county. In his old age he lost his eyesight and found his tongue. He accepted his affliction philosophically, and consoled himself by a flow of genial chatter never before heard from him. He attended cricket as long as his health would permit. With an acquired sense he was able to follow the play. 'He's middlin' the ball right.' But it was his delight in his last years to recall the old days. I asked him what he thought of Ranjitsinhji. 'He were a good bat were "Ranji". But I always fancied myself getting him leg before doin' that leg glance of his.' I tried again. 'What did you think of Trumper?' ''E were a good bat were Victor.' There was no advance of a 'good' bat in Wilfred's vocabulary of praise. Once, though, he let himself go. I asked him his opinion of Sidney Barnes as a bowler. 'The best of 'em today is half as good as Barnie.' He intended this as a compliment to the champions of today.

I last saw him as his daughter, Muriel, and her husband Tom

Burnley, led him out of Trent Bridge at the close of play of a Test match. More than fifty years ago he had first played for England, on this same ground, in 1899, when he was 21. Now he was going home to Canford Cliffs, Bournemouth, white stick in hand, arm in arm with his son-in-law, his face ruddy after hours sitting and listening to cricket, and whether he knew it or not, himself a permanent part of the game's history and traditions.

(Wisden 1974)

WODEHOUSE, SIR PELHAM GRENVILLE, the famous novelist who died in hospital on Long Island on February 14, 1975, at the age of 93, had been a member of the Dulwich College XI in 1899 and 1900. He was godfather of M. G. Griffith, the late Captain of Sussex.

(Wisden 1976)

BEDSER, ALEC, who died in June, 1981, aged 33, in a motor accident in Johannesburg, was a right-arm medium-paced bowler who played for Border in the Currie Cup in 1971–72. Like his twin brother, Eric (they were named after the famous English cricketing twins), Alec was a distinguished all-round sportsman. Another car accident, several years earlier, had curtailed his cricket career.

(Wisden 1982)

BADER, GROUP CAPT. SIR DOUGLAS, CBE, DSO, DFC, the famous airman who died on September 5, 1982, aged 72, was captain of St Edward's School, Oxford, in 1928. A good attacking 41 bat and a useful fast-medium bowler, he later played for the RAF and in 1931 made 65, the top score, for them against the Army, a fixture which in those days had first-class status. He gained greater distinction at rugger, and at the time of the accident the following winter which cost him his legs he was in the running for an England cap.

(Wisden 1983)

ACHONG, ELLIS EDGAR ('PUSS'), died in Port-of-Spain, Trinidad, on August 29, 1986, aged 82. A left-arm spin bowler, he was the first cricketer of Chinese extraction to play Test cricket, appearing for West Indies in six matches against England and taking eight wickets at 47.25. Chosen to tour England in 1933, he played in all three Tests but with limited success, and in all first-class matches that season took 71 wickets. Essentially an orthodox slow left-armer, at Manchester he had Robins stumped by a ball which, bowled with a wrist-spinner's action, turned into the right-hander from the off and gave rise to the use in England of the word 'chinaman' to describe such a delivery. After 1935 he played in the Lancashire leagues until 1951, and having returned to live in Trinidad he stood as an umpire in the 1953–54 Port-of-Spain Test between West Indies and England. In all first-class matches he took 110 wickets at 30.23, his best figures being seven for 73 for Trinidad against British Guiana in 1932–33.

(Wisden 1987)

CAESAR, WILLIAM CECIL, who died on April 5, 1988, at the age of 88, made four appearances in first-class cricket as an amateur, the first being for Surrey in 1922, when he was a distinctly quick right-arm bowler. His next three were not until 1946 and all for Somerset. This gap of twenty-four years between appearances has only once been exceeded. Caesar's best performance with the ball was four for 59 against Leicestershire at Melton Mowbray in his first match for Somerset, and in all he took ten wickets at 25.20 apiece. As a tailender he was unable to make more than a negligible contribution. Caesar was a very fine soccer player, an amateur international, who at one time or another turned out for Darlington, Fulham, Walsall and Brentford.

(*Wisden*) 1989

O'REILLY, WILLIAM JOSEPH, OBE, who died in a Sydney hospital on October 6, 1992, aged 86, was probably the greatest spin bowler the game has ever produced. Bill 'Tiger' O'Reilly was unquestionably one of cricket's great figures: as a player, as a character and later as a writer on the game. His cricket was proof that spin bowling was not necessarily a gentle art. He was 6ft 2in tall, gripped the ball in his enormous right hand and released it at a pace that could be almost fast-medium. It would then bounce ferociously on the hard pitches of his time and, on occasion, knock wicket-keepers off their feet. He bowled leg-breaks and, especially, top-spinners and googlies, backed up by an intimidating manner. Jack Fingleton said he was 'a flurry of limbs, fire and steel-edged temper'. It has been suggested that his action and the general commotion before delivery were born of a deep sense of frustration at not being able to bowl fast enough to knock the batsman down. Off the field, his gruffness was mitigated by his intelligence, erudition, wit and twinkling eyes.

He played 27 Test matches and took 144 wickets – 102 of them Englishmen and the vital wicket of Walter Hammond ten times –

averaging 22.59. But his figures have to be judged by the fact that all but one of his Tests came in the 1930s, when other bowlers were dominated by batsmen to an unprecedented extent. No one ever dominated O'Reilly. Even when England made 903 at The Oval in 1938, he bowled 85 overs and finished with figures of three for 178. And before that, he had secured the Ashes by taking five for 66 and five for 56 at Headingley.

O'Reilly was born in White Cliffs in the New South Wales bush into a large Irish family on December 20, 1905. His father was a small-town schoolmaster and young Bill was above average at several sports, including tennis, athletics and rugby. Cricket was harder to arrange. According to Jack Fingleton in *Cricket Crisis*, the four O'Reilly brothers played with a gum-wood bat and a piece of banksia root chiselled down to make a ball. Since the others were older, Bill inevitably bowled more than he batted. The brothers also cuffed him a lot, possibly because he was starting to show them up. In 1917 the family moved to Wingello. When he played his first match for Wingello Juniors, the team walked to the opposition's ground seven miles away in Tallong, with their dogs chasing rabbits along the way. In 1919, he went to the high school in the larger town of Goulburn, where he concentrated on his athletics as much as his cricket. And when he went to the teachers' college at Sydney University in his late teens he was more interested in such events as the hop, step and jump, in which he held the state record. According to Fingleton's account he would probably have been lost to cricket had he not been asked to make up the numbers in a Sydney junior match and, with a method that at first made everyone giggle, whipped out the opposition.

In the summer of 1925–26, the young O'Reilly, by now an
44 undergraduate at the teachers' college in Sydney University, met

the man whose destiny was to be linked with his for ever. O'Reilly's own account of this remains a classic. He was passing through Bowral Station on his way home to Wingello for his summer holiday when he heard his name being called down the platform. He put his head out of the carriage window and was told to get out at once: Wingello were playing at Bowral and needed him.

'How was I to know that I was about to cross swords with the greatest cricketer that ever set foot on a cricket field? He didn't have it all his own way, let me tell you. Well, not for the first couple of overs, anyway.' By the close of play, 17-year-old Don Bradman was 234 not out. The match resumed a week later, according to the local custom. 'The sun shone, the birds sang sweetly and the flowers bloomed as never before. I bowled him first ball with a leg-break which came from the leg-stump to hit the off bail. Suddenly cricket was the best game in the whole wide world.'

In 1926–27 O'Reilly was chosen for the New South Wales state practice squad on the strength of one match for North Sydney. A year later he made his first-class début against the New Zealanders. But teachers in New South Wales work for the state rather than an individual school and the newly-qualified O'Reilly was despatched to three different bush towns. This may have cost him the chance of a Test against England in 1928–29 and, very probably, a tour in 1930. He was transferred back to Sydney in time for the 1931–32 season and after four more matches made his début for Australia. He performed quietly in a match in which Bradman scored 299 not out and Grimmett took 14 wickets, but he had arrived.

In the 1932–33 Bodyline series he took 27 wickets, without anyone noticing much, given what else was happening. In the series in England in 1934 he took 28 wickets, including seven in an innings twice. At Trent Bridge he won the match with seven for 54, achieved by what *Wisden* called 'clever variation in flight and pace combined with spin off the worn turf'. In blazing heat at Old Trafford, he transformed the game in an over which England began at 68 for no wicket. Walters was caught at forward short leg off the first ball, Wyatt bowled middle stump by the second and Hammond, after glancing a four off the third, was bowled by the fourth. Hendren and Leyland recaptured the initiative and England declared at 627 for nine but O'Reilly finished with seven for 189. He took 109 wickets on the tour, including nine for 38 against Somerset. He went back to Australia and suddenly announced his retirement. He had married in 1933, had a daughter and was anxious about his teaching career. However, Sydney Grammar School offered him a job that enabled him to play on. He toured South Africa in 1935–36 and took 27 wickets again, 25 in the great series against England in 1936–37 and 22 back in England in 1938, despite the unforgiving wickets ('dosed up to the eyeballs', said O'Reilly) of Trent Bridge and The Oval.

He played only one more Test, the one-off game against New Zealand at Wellington in March 1946 when he was already 40. The opposition barely beat his age: they were bowled out for 42 and 54 and O'Reilly took five for 14 and three for 19. It was the eleventh time he had taken five in an innings in Tests. O'Reilly then began writing on cricket for the *Sydney Morning Herald* with a muscular, very Australian prose style flavoured with wit and imagery ('You can smell the gum-leaves off him', he wrote of one country boy just starting with Queensland). Until he finally retired in 1988, he was as revered in Australian press boxes as he had been on the field. His opinions often came more from the heart than the head, especially if it was a question of attacking the selectors for playing safe and ignoring a young player, most especially a young leg-spinner. But he was consistent, loved quality and hated one-day cricket ('hit-and-giggle') which he generally refused to watch. He was hot-blooded and humorous, which perhaps explains why his relationship with the cooler Bradman is believed to have been based on intense mutual respect rather than the profoundest form of Australian mateship. While Sir Donald walked the corridors of cricketing power O'Reilly was the rumbustious backbencher.

His last few years were rendered miserable by illness, including the loss of a leg. But he was blessed with a marriage to Molly that lasted fifty-nine years. In his career he took 774 wickets at 16.60 and was successful at every level: playing for North Sydney and St George, he topped the Sydney Grade averages twelve times and took 962 wickets at 9.44. He took a wicket every 49 balls in his first-class career and it was said he never bowled a wide. His batting was left-handed, hard-hitting and occasionally stubborn (1,655 runs at 13.13); he never quite forgave himself for getting out at Lord's in 1934 when he might have saved the follow-on, in which case he rather than Verity would have had use of a rain-affected wicket. He did save the follow-on by making 30 not out at Old Trafford in the next Test. Future generations will have to judge the greatness of his bowling on the fragments of film that survive and the written descriptions, of which R. C. Robertson-Glasgow's may stand as definitive:

As with those more florid opponents of legendary heroes, there seemed to be more arms than Nature or the rules allow. During the run-up, a sort of fierce galumph, the right forearm worked like a piston; at delivery the head was ducked low as if to butt the batsman on to his stumps. But it didn't take long to see the greatness; the control of leg-break, top-spinner and googly; the change of pace and trajectory without apparent change in action; the scrupulous length; the vitality; and, informing and rounding all, the brain to diagnose what patient required what treatment.

When O'Reilly died, Bradman said he was the greatest bowler he had ever faced or watched.

(*Wisden* 1993)

FARGUS, REV. ARCHIBALD HUGH CONWAY, who died on October 6, 1963, aged 84, has been obituarised before in *Wisden*. However, this was forty-eight years before his death. The 1915 edition said Fargus had gone down with the *Monmouth*, the ship on which he was acting-chaplain, in action in the Pacific. But he had missed a train and failed to rejoin the ship. Fargus, whose father Hugh Conway was a well-known Victorian author, won a Cambridge Blue in 1900 and 1901 and played fifteen games for Gloucestershire. His actual death was not reported in the Almanack.

(from the supplementary obituaries in *Wisden* 1994)

MAJOR, JOHN, who died at Wakefield, Yorkshire on December 31, 1930, aged 69, came to public attention as a professional right-handed batsman with an excellent style while playing Sussex Colts matches in 1888. However, he would have been a very elderly colt. Contemporary references said he was born in 1865; his birth certificate shows that he was actually four years older. Major played eleven first-class games for Sussex, averaging 17.28, scoring 106 against Gloucestershire in 1889. He played soccer for West Bromwich Albion and later joined the Warwickshire staff. On his death certificate, he was described as a 'former general labourer'.

(from the supplementary obituaries in *Wisden* 1994)

MOSS, REV. REGINALD HEBER, who died on March 19, 1956, aged 88, played for Oxford, winning his Blue in 1889, and had one further first-class game for Liverpool and District in 1893. He then played one Championship match for Worcestershire, against Gloucestershire at Worcester, as a 57-year-old in 1925 and took a wicket and two catches. He was then rector of Icomb, near Stow-on-the-Wold. The gap of thirty-two years between first-class appearances is a record.

(from the supplementary obituaries in Wisden 1994)

CRISP, ROBERT JAMES, DSO, MC, who died in Essex on March 3, 1994, aged 82, was one of the most extraordinary men ever to play Test cricket. His cricket, which is only a fraction of the story, was explosive enough: he is the only bowler to have taken four wickets in four balls twice. Born in Calcutta, he was educated in Rhodesia and, after taking nine for 64 for Western Province against Natal in 1933–34, which included his second set of four in four, was chosen for the South Africans' 1935 tour of England. He took 107 wickets on the tour at a brisk fast-medium, including five for 99 in the Old Trafford Test. Crisp played four further Tests against Australia in 1935–36 and appeared eight times for Worcestershire in 1938 without ever achieving a huge amount.

But it is astonishing that he ever found a moment for such a time-consuming game as cricket. He was essentially an adventurer – he had just climbed Kilimanjaro when he got news that he was wanted for the 1935 tour – with something of an attention span problem. Like other such characters, his defining moment came in the Second World War when he was an outstanding but turbulent tank commander, fighting his own personal war against better-armoured Germans in Greece and North Africa. He had six tanks blasted from under him in a month but carried on fighting and was awarded the DSO 'for outstanding ability and great gallantry'. However, he annoyed authority so much that General Montgomery intervened personally and prevented him being given a Bar a year later; his second honour was downgraded to an MC. Crisp was mentioned in despatches four times before being invalided out in Normandy. The King asked if his bowling would be affected. 'No, sire,' he is alleged to have replied. 'I was hit in the head.'

Crisp never did play again and found that the tedium of peacetime presented him with a problem far harder than anything offered by the Germans. He was briefly a journalist for a succession of newspapers, and went back to South Africa where he founded the now firmly-established paper for blacks, *Drum*. But he wanted a magazine about tribal matters rather than something appealing to urban blacks and rapidly fell out with his proprietor. He returned to England, tried mink farming and, for an unusually long time by Crisp standards, worked as a leader-writer on the *East Anglian Daily Times*. While there he wrote two accounts of his war exploits, *Brazen Chariots* (1957) and *The Gods Were Neutral* (1960). Then he suddenly left and lived in a Greek hut for a year. Told he had incurable cancer, he spent a year walking round Crete, selling accounts to the *Sunday Express*. He died with a copy of the *Sporting Life* on his lap, reportedly having just lost a £20 bet, a risk-taker to the last. Crisp's 276 career wickets came at an average of only 19.88, but statistics are absurd for such a man.

(*Wisden* 1995)

PENGUIN 60s

Biography

DIRK BOGARDE · *Coming of Age*
ANTHONY BURGESS · *Childhood*
RICHARD ELLMANN · *The Trial of Oscar Wilde*
MARIANNE FAITHFULL · *Year One*
KATHARINE HEPBURN · *Little Me*
BARRY HUMPHRIES · *Less is More Please*
LAURIE LEE · *To War in Spain*
BLAKE MORRISON · *Camp Cuba*
VLADIMIR NABOKOV · *Now Remember*
LYTTON STRACHEY · *Florence Nightingale*

Cookery

LINDSEY BAREHAM · *The Little Book of Big Soups*
ELIZABETH DAVID · *Peperonata and Other Italian Dishes*
KEITH FLOYD · *Hot and Spicy Floyd*
JANE GRIGSON · *Puddings*
SOPHIE GRIGSON · *From Sophie's Table*
CLAUDIA RODEN · *Ful Medames and Other Vegetarian Dishes*
HELGE RUBINSTEIN · *Chocolate Parfait*
NIGEL SLATER · *30-Minute Suppers*
RICK STEIN · *Fresh from the Sea*
MARGARET VISSER · *More Than Meets the Eye*

Travel

KAREN BLIXEN · *From the Ngong Hills*
ALEXANDER FRATER · *Where the Dawn Comes Up like Thunder*
PATRICK LEIGH FERMOR · *Loose As the Wind*
JAN MORRIS · *Scenes from Havian Life*
REDMOND O'HANLON · *A River in Borneo*
MARK SHAND · *Elephant Tales*
PAUL THEROUX · *Slow Trains to Simla*
COLIN THUBRON · *Samarkand*
MARK TULLY · *Beyond Purdah*
GAVIN YOUNG · *Something of Samoa*

READ MORE IN PENGUIN

For complete information about books available from Penguin and how to order them, please write to us at the appropriate address below. Please note that for copyright reasons the selection of books varies from country to country.

IN THE UNITED KINGDOM: Please write to *Dept. EP, Penguin Books Ltd, Bath Road, Harmondsworth, Middlesex UB7 0DA.*

IN THE UNITED STATES: Please write to *Consumer Sales, Penguin USA, P.O. Box 999, Dept. 17109, Bergenfield, New Jersey 07621-0120.* VISA and MasterCard holders call 1-800-253-6476 to order Penguin titles.

IN CANADA: Please write to *Penguin Books Canada Ltd, 10 Alcorn Avenue, Suite 300, Toronto, Ontario M4V 3B2.*

IN AUSTRALIA: Please write to *Penguin Books Australia Ltd, P.O. Box 257, Ringwood, Victoria 3134.*

IN NEW ZEALAND: Please write to *Penguin Books (NZ) Ltd, Private Bag 102902, North Shore Mail Centre, Auckland 10.*

IN INDIA: Please write to *Penguin Books India Pvt Ltd, 706 Eros Apartments, 56 Nehru Place, New Delhi 110 019.*

IN THE NETHERLANDS: Please write to *Penguin Books Netherlands bv, Postbus 3507, NL-1001 AH Amsterdam.*

IN GERMANY: Please write to *Penguin Books Deutschland GmbH, Metzlerstrasse 26, 60594 Frankfurt am Main.*

IN SPAIN: Please write to *Penguin Books S. A., Bravo Murillo 19, 1º B, 28015 Madrid.*

IN ITALY: Please write to *Penguin Italia s.r.l., Via Felice Casati 20, I–20124 Milano.*

IN FRANCE: Please write to *Penguin France S. A., 17 rue Lejeune, F–31000 Toulouse.*

IN JAPAN: Please write to *Penguin Books Japan, Ishikiribashi Building, 2–5–4, Suido, Bunkyo-ku, Tokyo 112.*

IN GREECE: Please write to *Penguin Hellas Ltd, Dimocritou 3, GR–106 71 Athens.*

IN SOUTH AFRICA: Please write to *Longman Penguin Southern Africa (Pty) Ltd, Private Bag X08, Bertsham 2013.*